Health and Safety in
HORSE RIDING ESTABLISHMENTS

HSE BOOKS

© Crown copyright 1993
Applications for reproduction should
be made to HMSO
First published 1993

ISBN 0 7176 0632 5

CONTENTS

Introduction 1

Legal duties 3
Duties of employers to employees 3
Consultation with employees 3
Health and safety records and documentation 4
Duties of employers to people not in their employment 4
Contractors 5   Duties of self-employed people 5
Duties of people in charge of premises 6
Duties of employees 6

Management of health and safety 7

Training 9
General 9   Instructors 10

Manual handling 13
Making an assessment 13   Reducing the risk of injury 13
Handling techniques 15   Safe stacking of bales 15

Accidents and incidents 18
Notification of injuries and dangerous occurrences 18
Notification of reportable diseases 21   Record keeping 21
Summary table 22   First aid 23

Occupational health 24
Control of Substances Hazardous to Health Regulations 1988 24
Hazards associated with dusts 26   Zoonoses 28
Other risks to workers 30   Pesticides 30

Veterinary treatment 32
Disposal of medicines 33 Restraining the horse 33

Environment and welfare 34
Stabling 34   Collecting yard 37 Riding areas or manege 37
Indoor schools 38 Grazing paddocks 38   Visitors' areas 38
General horse handling 39   General housekeeping 39
Children 40   Facilities for employees 40

Tack 42
The saddle 42   Stirrup leathers 42   Stirrup irons 42
Bridles 45   Bits 45

Riding and road safety 46
Rider safety 46   Personal protective equipment (PPE) 46
Rider dress 48   Road safety 50

Electrical safety 53
Fixed electrical installations 53   Electrical equipment 54

Machinery 56
Approaching dangerous parts - power isolation 56
Tractors 56   Grass cutters 58   Chaff cutters 58
Oat rollers 58   Horse walkers 58
Steam/water pressure cleaners 59

Appendix 1	Horse behaviour 60	
Appendix 2	Self-audit check-list 63	
Appendix 3	Advice on safety policy statement 65	
Appendix 4	Factors/questions when making an assessment of manual handling operations 67	
Appendix 5	Example Form F2508 for reporting injuries and dangerous occurrences 69	
Appendix 6	Example Form F2508A for reporting cases of disease 70	
Appendix 7	Useful addresses and contacts 71	

References and further reading 72

INTRODUCTION

1 The majority of accidents at riding establishments are associated with horses themselves, either from riding or handling. Horses are unpredictable and work involving them can never be totally without risks. The proprietor of the riding establishment should devise safe systems of work to help minimise the risks. Throughout this booklet the word 'horse' includes pony and other equines.

2 The booklet is intended for proprietors and managers of riding establishments and also for employees and safety representatives. It describes the main risks associated with handling horses, the machinery, equipment, substances and work practices found in riding establishments and what should be considered to safeguard the health and safety of both workers and visitors to the premises. It has been produced by the Health and Safety Executive Local Authority Unit after consultation with the British Horse Society and the Association of British Riding Schools.

3 The guidance contained in this booklet is *not* mandatory. It does set out information on the responsibilities of employers and employees under health and safety legislation. However, the advice on implementing safe systems of work is guidance *only*, and employers may take alternative effective steps if they wish.

LEGAL DUTIES

4   The Health and Safety at Work etc Act 1974 applies to all people at work, employers, self-employed and employees. The legislation protects not only people at work, but also the health and safety of the general public who may be affected by work activities.

Duties of employers to employees

5   Employers have a general duty under the Act to ensure so far as is reasonably practicable the health, safety and welfare at work of all their employees. This duty includes:

(a)   providing and maintaining plant, machinery and systems of work that are safe and without risks to health;

(b)   ensuring that articles and substances are used, handled, stored and transported safely and without risks to health;

(c)   providing the necessary information, instruction, training and supervision to ensure the health and safety at work of all employees;

(d)   maintaining a workplace that is safe and without risks to health, including safe entrance and exit;

(e)   providing and maintaining a working environment which is safe, without risks to health and with adequate welfare facilities and arrangements for employees' welfare at work.

Consultation with employees

6   Good health and safety cannot be achieved without the co-operation of employees. The role of the safety representative is therefore a valuable way of communicating with employees and also in helping managers to identify and tackle problems. If they are appointed by a recognised trade union, safety representatives have statutory rights, for example to be consulted on matters affecting health and safety; to carry out inspections; and to request the setting up of a safety committee.

Health and safety records and documentation

7   Employers with five or more employees are required to prepare a written statement of their general policy, organisation and arrangements for the health and safety at work of their employees. The statement and any revision of it should be brought to the attention of all the employees. Employers should record significant findings of their risk assessment. This record should represent an effective statement of hazards and risks which then leads management to take the relevant actions to protect health and safety. They should also record their arrangements for health and safety.

8   These duties are supplemented by a wide variety of more specific regulations made under the Act. Together they form a network of legal requirements designed to achieve the main objective set out in section 2 of the Act.

Duties of employers to people not in their employment

9   Employers and self-employed people have a responsibility for the health and safety of members of the public, self-employed people or contractors' employees working with them who may be affected by work activities under their control. In fact, employers who share their workplace with another employer or self-employed person or who have other employer's staff working in their workplace, have a duty to co-operate and exchange information on health and safety.

10   The range of people that need to be considered depends on the nature of the business. Those who could be affected by the business either in the normal course of events or if things went wrong could include:

(a)   horse riders/customers/clients;

(b)   contractors and their employees working on the premises, for example farrier and vet;

(c)   users of facilities, machinery and spectators;

(d) visitors to the premises;

(e) people living, working or passing close to the premises;

(f) people working for you but not classed as employees such as youngsters helping out at busy periods;

(g) pupils, students, trainees and any others who may be on the premises for any length of time. Trainees on the Government Training Schemes on work experience count as employees of the immediate provider of their training at workplaces, for the purpose of health and safety legislation.

Some of the people who might be at risk could be children or people with a disability, who may be especially vulnerable. People can be absent-minded, careless, inquisitive, or simply unaware of a potential hazard (particularly horse behaviour) which may seem obvious to an experienced person, and this should be taken into account.

Contractors

11 All hired contractors have their own duties to comply with relevant health and safety legislation, but they need to be given the information about the premises to ensure their health and safety, eg whether asbestos is present. Employers should enquire about the contractor's own procedures so that they will not endanger themselves or resident staff. Where possible, contractors should work in an area segregated from the normal running of the establishment. Noisy equipment such as electric drills should, whenever possible, be kept away from areas where there are horses.

Duties of self-employed people

12 Self-employed people have a specific duty not to create risks to the health and safety of other people or themselves. They also have other duties similar to those for employers.

Duties of people in charge of premises

13 If non-domestic premises are made available to non-employees as a place of work where they may use plant or substances provided for their use there, then the person in control of the premises has a duty to ensure that the premises and any plant or substances provided in those premises, eg ladders, electrical equipment do not create a risk to health and safety. The extent of the responsibilities of individuals depends on how far they control the premises. (A local authority enforcement officer from the local Environmental Health Department will be able to give advice.)

Duties of employees

14 The legal duties of employees include:

(a) taking reasonable care of their own health and safety and that of others who may be affected by what they do or omit to do at work;

(b) co-operating with their employer on health and safety matters;

(c) not interfering with or misusing anything provided in the interests of health, safety and welfare of themselves or others;

(d) informing their employer of any shortcoming in the health and safety arrangements, even when no immediate dangers exist.

15 Not all health and safety regulations are relevant to all types of work activity. However, the Management of Health and Safety Regulations 1992[1] *do* apply to all work activities. They put further detail on those duties of employers, the self-employed and employees mentioned above. In effect they make much clearer what is required to comply with the general duties of the Act itself. There is also a range of Approved Codes of Practice and other guidance to help employers understand how to carry out their duties; and these are listed where relevant.

MANAGEMENT OF HEALTH AND SAFETY

16 Good health and safety in the workplace does not happen of its own accord, eg safe systems of work have to be implemented, staff trained, machinery and equipment maintained in good condition etc. In other words, health and safety has to be managed, as with any other part of the business.

17 Working to ensure health and safety is not only a legal requirement but also makes good economic sense. Employers can ill afford the loss of a valuable member of staff with back pain caused by poor lifting technique or an injury resulting from a preventable fall.

18 Risk assessments play a major role in maintaining and improving the standards of health and safety. The Management of Health and Safety at Work Regulations 1992[1] requires employers to assess the risks to employees and any others who may be affected by their undertaking. The assessments should be seen as a means of arriving at the right decision on how to control a risk. They are not an end in themselves and in many cases measures to control the risk can be obvious and easy to implement. Trivial risks can usually be ignored as can risks arising from routine activities associated with life in general (unless the work activity is especially relevant to those risks). Many aspects of running a riding establishment involve taking decisions which can affect health and safety. The value of a risk assessment is in allowing all the relevant factors to be considered before arriving at a decision. Some risk assessments may be simple and arise directly from observation, eg whether the tack is safe to use. Others may be more complex and could include staff training needs; types of equipment, how it is used, and by whom; suitability of horses and ponies and risks to staff, clients, visitors, etc as a result of contractors working at the premises. Specific risk assessments already carried out under other health and safety legislation, eg COSHH and manual handling regulations do not need to be repeated or duplicated; they will form part of the overall risk assessment. Recording significant risks gives management the opportunity of assessing how well the risks are controlled.

Appropriate arrangements should be considered for putting into practice the preventative and protective measures that follow from the risk assessment. Effective health and safety arrangements will cover planning, organisation, control, monitoring and review.

19 Keeping records in some cases is a legal requirement and in others a convenient and sensible way to manage health and safety. The following list could help when deciding which areas of activity need to be reviewed:

(a) maintenance and service records for all equipment and machines;

(b) staff and trainee training records;

(c) electrical equipment and installation certificate;

(d) specific assessments, eg control of substances hazardous to health, protective clothing etc;

(e) accident/incident records;

(f) in-house or self-audit inspection records;

(g) fire appliances, alarms service and test records.

If records are kept, they need to be accurate, up to date and easily retrievable.

20 Monitoring the operation of the safety policy is one way of ensuring that people are adhering to procedures. All accidents and near misses should be investigated to find out why they occurred and how they can be prevented in the future. An accident investigation may show that a change of procedure is necessary.

TRAINING

General

21 The Management of Health and Safety at Work Regulations 1992[1] require employers to take into account their employees' capabilities, as regards health and safety, when giving them tasks to do, eg previous training, knowledge and experience. Employers should also ensure their employees are provided with adequate health and safety training.

22 Training is an important way of achieving health and safety competence and helps to convert information into safe working practices. The Joint National Horse Education and Training Council are responsible for developing standards of competence upon which the National Vocational Qualification (NVQ) in England and Wales or the Scottish Vocational Education Council (SCOTVEC) are based. (See Appendix 7 for the address of the Joint National Horse Education and Training Council).

23 New employees (including volunteers and casual staff) should receive induction training on health and safety, including arrangements for first aid, emergency procedures, fire and evacuation. The needs of young workers should also be given particular attention. However, training is needed at all levels, including top management.

24 Risk assessments should identify where specific training is required, for example manual handling, using hazardous substances. Training needs may change when employees transfer or take on new responsibilities, or staff return to work after long periods of absence, or there is a change in equipment or systems of work or procedures.

25 The competence of staff should be monitored where lack of job knowledge and skills can adversely affect health and safety, and any necessary update or refresher training provided. Special attention may need to be given to employees who deputise for others. Their skills are likely to be underdeveloped and they may need more help

in understanding the health and safety issues. Staff who work only at weekends may also have training needs and can easily be overlooked. Accidents and ill health can often be traced to poorly informed decisions through lack of training. Training can improve job performance, and it is sensible to keep a record of significant training events.

Instructors

26 It is recommended that only instructors who can demonstrate their competence and have obtained appropriate qualifications from equestrian organisations are employed (see Appendix 7).

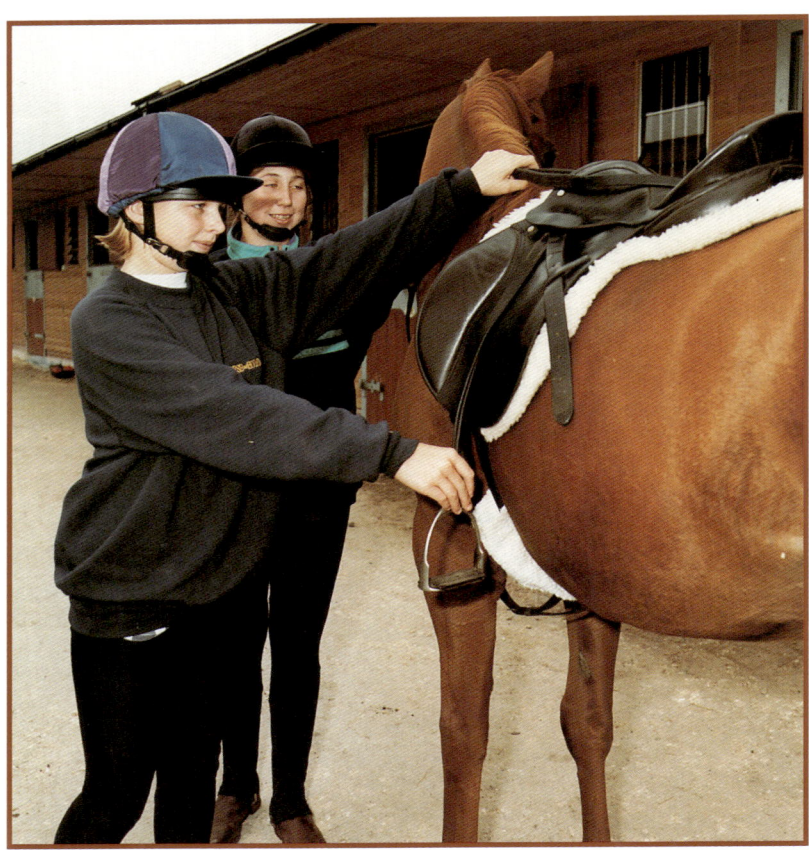

27 The Riding Establishment Act 1964 defines an approved certificate as any one of the certificates issued by the British Horse Society, namely the British Horse Society Assistant Instructor, Instructors Certificate and Fellowship or Fellowship of the Institute of the Horse. If certificates from other equestrian organisations are to be accepted then they should be of equal standing to these and be appropriate for the activities carried out by the riding establishment. Instructors who have no formal qualifications, but are able to demonstrate their competence by many years' experience and the ability to run a business properly, are deemed to meet the necessary standards.

28 The Joint National Horse Education and Training Council are responsible for developing standards of competence. An indication of competence is completion of a relevant element or unit of competence within an appropriate National Vocational Qualification (NVQ) or Scottish Vocational Education Council (SCOTVEC). The British Horse Society holds a register of instructors who are held to be competent by way of their qualifications, hold insurance and have agreed to follow a Code of Conduct.

29 It is recommended that no one under the age of 16 should be left in control of an establishment, be permitted to instruct or be in control of a lesson or ride.

Instructor:student ratios

30 An assessment to determine the competence instructor:student ratios will include:

(a) the experience and qualifications of the instructors;

(b) the experience and ability of the student(s);

(c) the temperament and experience of the horse;

(d) the type of lesson being undertaken.

MANUAL HANDLING

31 Almost one third of all accidents reported to HSE and local authorities each year arise from manual handling. In riding establishments there will be a range of manual handling tasks, from lifting water buckets to aiding people to mount horses. Sprains and strains of backs and limbs are often sustained from manual handling and lifting. The injury may also be a result of cumulative damage often sustained over a considerable period, which can result in physical impairment or even permanent disability. Sprains and strains occur when bodily force is applied incorrectly. Poor posture is often a contributory factor.

32 The Manual Handling Operations Regulations 1992[2] require employers to take reasonably practicable steps to avoid manual handling activities where there is a risk of injury. Where such manual handling cannot be avoided, the employer should make an assessment and take appropriate measures to remove or reduce the risk of injury. Handling includes pulling and pushing.

Making an assessment

33 When making an assessment, there are four elements to be considered, the task, the load, the working environment and individual capability. (See Appendix 4 for a check-list to aid assessment.) It should be possible to complete the majority of assessments in house. The publication *Manual Handling*[2] will help when this task is undertaken. Once the risks have been identified and assessed, suitable measures should be taken whenever appropriate to remove or reduce the risk of injury.

Reducing the risk of injury

34 *The task*. It should not be assumed that a particular manual handling operation is unavoidable, because it has always been the practice. For example carrying bales of hay when a trolley or wheelbarrow could be used, or taking the horse to the hay rather

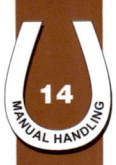

than the other way round. Small water buckets could be used to fill large buckets. The use of hosepipes can also reduce the need to carry water buckets long distances. Care should be taken to ensure that the hosepipe is positioned so as not to become a tripping hazard. Fatigue increases the likelihood of manual handling injuries, therefore the number and length of rest or recovery periods are important. Work should be organised, where practicable, so that manual handling tasks are spread throughout the working shift. This allows staff longer recovery periods between the manual handling activities. Staffing levels will affect workloads and rest and recovery periods.

35 *The load.* Loads will vary by size, weight, shape, fragility, stability, etc. Some may be difficult to grasp. Others may be sharp. The best way of handling the load considering the circumstances should be determined. There are additional complications when handling animals. The load lacks rigidity, there is particular concern on the part of the handler to avoid hurting them and to complicate matters the load will often have a mind of its own. These factors are likely to increase the risk of injury to the handler as compared with handling an inanimate load of similar weight and shape. Where appropriate, handling aids which restrain the animal and assist the task being performed should be used. Mounting blocks should be used in preference to giving a 'leg-up'. A bridle will help to reduce the strain on the handler when leading a strong horse.

36 *The working environment.* Heavy items stored at high levels or lifting in confined areas require consideration. For example, saddle racks placed at high levels may cause problems as some saddles are heavy and difficult to lift, and heavy items falling from a height can cause injuries to people. Uneven and slippery floors can also put extra strain on the handler. For outdoor workers the extremes of temperature or wind can affect their lifting capabilities.

37 *Individual capability.* Both the age and fitness of staff are important. The assessment should be updated to take account of the natural ageing process, injury, ill health, pregnancy etc. In general the lifting strength of women as a group is less than that of men but

there is considerable overlap, some women can deal safely with greater loads than some men. An individual's physical capacity varies with age, typically climbing until the early twenties and declining gradually from the mid forties. Therefore the risk of manual handling injuries may be somewhat higher for employees in their teens or in their fifties and sixties, though again the range of individual capability is large and the benefits of experience and maturity should not be overlooked.

Handling techniques

38 *The development of good handling techniques is no substitute for other risk reduction steps* such as improving the working environment, but it will form a very valuable addition to them. It requires both training and practice. Ideally, training should be tailored to the particular handling operation likely to be undertaken and be carried out in conditions that are as realistic and relevant as possible to the job. The check-list overleaf (Figure 1) illustrates some important points.

Safe stacking of bales

39 All work activities involving bale stacking and handling need to be assessed to find out the risks and to identify the steps needed to eliminate or reduce them. Many accidents result from handling misshapen or damaged bales and through badly formed stacks which are or become unstable in use. By ensuring that bales are well made, are a consistent size and shape and are well stacked, the risks can be greatly reduced. Everyone involved in the manual handling of bales should receive adequate supervision, instruction and training. Children should be kept away from bale stacks and any handling operations.

Figure 1 Manual handling check-list

- **Stop and think**.
  Plan the lift. Where is the load to be placed? Use appropriate handling aids if possible. Is help needed with the load?

- **Place the feet**.
  Stand with feet apart, giving a balanced and stable base for lifting. Place leading leg as far forward as is comfortable.

- **Adopt a good posture**.
  Bend the knees so that the hands are as nearly level with the waist as possible when grasping the load. Do not kneel or overflex the knees. Keep the back straight (tucking in the chin helps). Lean forward a little over the load if necessary to get a good grip. Keep shoulders level and facing in the same direction as the hips.

- **Get a firm grip**.
  Try to keep the arms within the boundary formed by the legs. The optimum position and nature of the grip depends on the circumstances and individual preference; but it must be secure. A hook grip is less fatiguing than keeping the fingers straight. If it is necessary to vary the grip as the lift proceeds, do this as smoothly as possible.

❑ **Don't jolt.** Carry out the lifting movement smoothly, keeping control of the load.

❑ **Move the feet.** Don't raise the trunk when turning to the side.

❑ **Keep close to the load**. Keep the load close to the trunk for as long as possible. Keep the heaviest side of the load next to the trunk. If a close approach to the load is not possible try sliding it towards you before attempting to lift it.

❑ **Put down, then adjust**. If precise positioning of the load is necessary, put it down first, then slide it into the desired position.

ACCIDENTS AND INCIDENTS

40 The Reporting of Injuries, Diseases and Dangerous Occurrences Regulations 1985 (RIDDOR) require employers, people in control of premises and in some cases the self-employed to report certain types of injury, occupational ill health and dangerous occurrences to their enforcing authority. In the case of riding establishments the enforcing authority is the local environmental health department. The following paragraphs give a summary of the requirements, but are by no means a comprehensive or exhaustive statement of law. More detailed information is provided in the HSE booklet HS(R)23 *Guide to the Reporting of Injuries, Diseases and Dangerous Occurrences Regulations 1985*[3].

Notification of injuries and dangerous occurrences

41 There are two ways in which injuries and incidents have to be reported to an enforcing authority and these depend on the severity and the potential for harm:

(a) (i) if someone dies or suffers a specified injury (see paragraph 42) in an accident arising from or in connection with work;
or
     (ii) there is a dangerous occurrence (see paragraph 43).

The employer should notify the enforcing authority immediately by the quickest practicable means, normally by telephone, and within seven days send a written report using form 2508. Form F2508 should be used to report injuries and dangerous occurrences. Form F2508A should be used for cases of disease. Appendices 5 and 6 reproduce the forms. These may be photocopied for your own use, or they can be purchased from HSE Books. Authorised report forms generated by a computerised accident recording system, several of which are commercially available, may also be used. Reports are required whether or not the person concerned is an employee.

(b) where an employee is off work or cannot carry out his or her normal duties for more than three consecutive days as a result of an

accident at work, this is also reportable and the employer has seven days in which to send a report to the enforcing authority.

Specified injuries

42 See check-list below for injuries which are required to be notified by the quickest practicable means (see also paragraph 41).

- fracture of the skull, spine or pelvis;

- fracture of any bone in the arm or wrist, but not a bone in the hand; or in the leg or ankle, but not a bone in the foot;

- amputation of a hand or foot, or a finger, thumb or toe, or any part of these if the joint or bone is completely severed;

- the loss of sight of an eye, a penetrating injury to an eye, or a chemical or hot metal burn to an eye;

- either injury (including burns) requiring immediate medical treatment, or loss of consciousness resulting in either case from an electric shock from any electrical circuit or equipment, whether or not due to direct contact;

- loss of consciousness resulting from lack of oxygen;

- either acute illness requiring treatment, or loss of consciousness, resulting in either case from absorption of any substance by inhalation, ingestion or through the skin;

- acute illness requiring medical treatment where there is reason to believe that this resulted from exposure to a pathogen or infected material;

- any other injury which results in the person injured being admitted immediately into hospital for more than 24 hours.

Dangerous occurrences

43 Certain dangerous occurrences are required to be reported and a full list is given in the booklet HS(R)23[3]. The most relevant to riding establishments are listed in the check-list below.

- the collapse of, overturning of, or failure of any lift, hoist or mobile powered access platform;

- explosion, collapse or bursting of any closed vessel, including a boiler or boiler tube, in which the internal pressure was above or below atmospheric pressure, which might have been liable to cause the death of, or injuries to any person, or which resulted in the stoppage of the plant involved for more than 24 hours;

- electrical short circuit or overload attended by fire or explosion which resulted in the stoppage of the plant involved for more than 24 hours, and might have been liable to cause death or injuries to any person;

- an explosion or fire occurring in any plant or place which resulted in the stoppage of that plant or suspension of normal work in that place for more than 24 hours, where such explosion or fire was due to the ignition of process materials, their by-products (including waste) or finished process;

- a collapse or partial collapse of any scaffold which is more than five metres high;

- any unintended collapse or partial collapse of:

    - any building or structure under construction, reconstruction, alteration or demolition involving a fall of more than five tonnes of material; or

    - any floor or wall of any building being used as a place of work, not being a building under construction, reconstruction, alteration or demolition.

Notification of reportable diseases

44 Where a person at work suffers from a reportable disease which is linked with specified work activities, the employer should immediately send a written report to the enforcing authority. This will be required only if the employer receives a written diagnosis of the disease made by a doctor; and the ill employee's current job involves a specified work activity.

45 The reportable diseases and specified work activities most relevant to riding establishments are:

(a) *occupational asthma*, caused by the dust from the handling and storage of barley, oats, rye, wheat or maize;

(b) *extrinsic alveolitis*, eg farmer's lung caused by the exposure to moulds or fungal spores in forage and bedding;

(c) *leptospirosis*, handling animals or work in places which are or may be infested by rats.

Certain public health diseases should be reported to the local environmental health department although not reportable under RIDDOR, eg dysentery, measles, mumps, rubella, tetanus.

Record keeping

46 The employer should keep a record of any reportable accidents and dangerous occurrences. These records will include the date and time of accident or occurrence; the name, occupation and nature of injury of the person affected; the place where the incident happened and a brief description of the circumstances. The employer should also keep a record of any reportable disease. These records will include the date of diagnosis of the disease; the occupation of the person affected and the name or nature of the disease. These records should be kept for at least three years.

Summary table

47 The following table shows typical accidents and gives details of whether or not they are reportable under RIDDOR.

Person involved	Accident details	Type of injury	Reportable under RIDDOR
Employee	Fell off ladder going into hayloft. Broke arm.	Major injury	Phone enforcing authority, send F2508 within seven days.
Client	Fell off ladder going into hayloft. Broke arm.	Major injury	Phone enforcing authority, send F2508 within seven days.
Employee	Fell off horse in manege. Banged head. Taken to hospital and detained for 24 hours. Returned to work the following day.	Major injury	Phone enforcing authority, send F2508 within seven days.
Client	Fell off horse in manege. Banged head. Taken to hospital and detained for 24 hours. Returned to work/school the following day.	Major injury	Phone enforcing authority, send F2508 within seven days.
Employee	Hurt back while lifting bale of hay. Off work for four days.	Over-3-day injury	Send F2508 within seven days to enforcing authority.
Employee	Hurt back while digging garden at home. Off work for four days. Accident happened at home.		Not reportable.
Client	Hurt back while lifting bale of hay. Off work for four days.	Not reportable.	Over-3-day injuries only applicable to employees.

48 With all accidents, if in doubt report it. Accidents which are not reportable will be filtered out at the enforcing authority. Reporting an accident does not suggest in any way that an offence has been committed, it is simply informing the enforcing authority that an accident has occurred at the premises. Failure to report an accident or disease described in RIDDOR is a criminal offence and may result in prosecution.

First aid

49 Under the Health and Safety (First Aid) Regulations 1981 workplaces should have first-aid provision. The form it should take depends on various factors, including the nature and degree of the hazards at work, whether there is shift working, what medical services are available, and the number of employees. The HSE booklet *First aid at work*[4] contains an Approved Code of Practice and guidance notes to help employers meet their obligations.

50 The minimum requirement for any workplace is that at all times when people are at work (including night shifts), there should be at least one appointed person who will take charge of the situation, eg by calling an ambulance. Ideally, appointed persons should have received training in emergency first aid. Although the Regulations refer only to provisions for employees it is recommended these are extended to cover clients. The nature of the work is likely to mean that at least one qualified first-aider will be needed. When activities take place away from the establishment base, there may be a case for extending to other staff, training in emergency aid. First-aid boxes and travelling first-aid kits should contain a sufficient quantity of suitable first-aid materials and nothing else.

51 Records of all accidents should be made and kept in a suitable, accessible place. Records should include at least the name of the casualty, date, time and circumstances of the accident, with details of the injury sustained and any treatment given. Employees or their representatives may wish to inspect these records at any time, they should therefore be kept in a suitable place so that they are easily available for inspection.

OCCUPATIONAL HEALTH

Control of Substances Hazardous to Health Regulations 1988

52 The Control of Substances Hazardous to Health Regulations 1988 (COSHH)[5] require employers to prevent or control exposure to hazardous substances at work. The Regulations were introduced to ensure that exposure to the hazardous substance is prevented, or where this is not reasonably practicable, adequately controlled. The employers' responsibility extends to the protection of any person who may be affected by the hazardous substance, and not just their employees.

53 The employer is required to carry out an assessment of the health risks faced by their employees, and to state the action they intend to take to prevent or control the exposure of his or her workforce to hazardous substances. Substances that are hazardous to health include those which are very toxic, toxic, harmful, irritant or corrosive. In a riding establishment, such substances include disinfectants, detergents, insecticides and veterinary products. Some of these may be hazardous substances and may create a risk to health if improperly used or mixed together. The Regulations also cover the exposure to harmful micro-organisms (such as Weil's disease and tetanus) and substantial quantities of dust from feed and bedding, and any other material, mixture or compound used at work, or arising from work activities, which can harm people's health.

54 The Regulations require all employers to:

(a) assess the risk to their employees and others from exposure to hazardous substances at work and so establish whether precautions are needed;

(b) introduce appropriate measures to prevent or control the risk for those substances where a risk has been identified which needs to be controlled;

(c) ensure that control measures are used and that equipment is properly maintained and procedures observed;

(d) where necessary, monitor the exposure of the workers and carry out an appropriateform of surveillance of their health;

(e) inform, instruct and train employees about the risks and the precautions to be taken.

Assessment

55 Employers should look at the work activities carried out and determine:

(a) what substances are present and in what form;

(b) what harmful effects are possible;

(c) where and how the substances are actually used and handled;

(d) whether harmful substances are given off or produced;

(e) whether a safer substitute material can be used;

(f) who could be affected, to what extent, for how long and under what circumstances;

(g) how likely is it that exposure will happen;

(h) whether precautions are required, such as protective clothing.

56 Certain information about products may be found on the label. If the information is not readily available from the label or supplier's advisory leaflet, then a data sheet for that product may be obtained from the supplier or manufacturer. They have a legal duty to supply such information. Many proprietary cleaning materials contain risk phrases such as 'avoid contact with skin'. In these circumstances, information from the

COSHH assessment would be used to make staff aware of the risk. Suitable training/instruction would then be given on how to use the product safely, and, where appropriate, protective gloves provided and staff instructed to use them.

57 The assessment will normally need to be written down for those substances which are hazardous to health. The assessment does not require all substances used in the workplace to be covered, eg soap, ink. Some chemicals which are relatively harmless on their own may become extremely hazardous when mixed, for example bleach and toilet cleaner. It is important that the employees are aware of this potential hazard. Substances used daily, which may not be labelled as hazardous may have the potential for causing health problems and should not be overlooked. For example, waste oil, used frequently as a substitute for hoof oil, can cause skin disorders such as acne.

58 Where health and safety information is contained on a label, the contents should not be decanted into smaller containers unless they are fully labelled in line with the original.

59 As with all management tasks, the process should be kept under review to ensure that appropriate control measures are being carried out and to check whether there have been any significant changes to working procedures, new materials etc which would merit reassessment. Practical guidance on COSHH is given in some detail in its associated Approved Codes of Practice[6].

Hazards associated with dusts

60 COSHH also covers dusts and micro-organisms. Exposure to these can cause or aggravate asthma and other allergic lung conditions. Substances causing these effects are called respiratory sensitisers. A respiratory sensitiser is a substance which, when inhaled, can trigger an irreversible allergic reaction in the respiratory system. Once this has occurred, subsequent exposure - even to minute amounts - may produce respiratory illness including:

(a) asthma attacks of wheezing, chest tightness and breathlessness resulting from constriction of the airways;

(b) Extrinsic Allergic Alveolitis (EAA) - breathlessness and flu-like symptoms. Continued exposure can lead to lung damage (eg farmer's lung);

(c) Rhinitis - runny nose, nasal congestion (eg hay fever).

Known respiratory sensitisers found in riding establishments are dusts found in horses' coats and moulds and fungal spores from hay, straw and animal feeds.

61 Symptoms may start within minutes of exposure or be delayed for several hours (eg occur at night) in which case their association with work may not be immediately recognised. However, relief from symptoms during rest days and holidays often points to an occupational cause. The earlier a sensitised person is removed from exposure, the greater the likelihood of avoiding serious damage to health. However, the potential to react to the sensitiser will stay with the individual for life. If exposure is allowed to continue, respiratory symptoms are likely to become progressively worse and may result in chronic disease, which may become so severe as to threaten life. Further information is given in the leaflet *Respiratory sensitisers: a guide for employers*[7].

Assessing the risk

62 Your COSHH assessment should cover at least the following questions for each substance:

(a) What is its potential to cause respiratory sensitisation?

(b) Is it likely to become airborne, eg grooming, putting straw bed down?

(c) Who is likely to be exposed, to what concentration, for how long and how often?

(d) What arrangements are needed for preventing exposure or if that is not practicable, securing and maintaining adequate control of exposure, monitoring, health surveillance, information, instruction, training?

Controlling exposure

63 Do not create more dust than necessary when working. Increase ventilation, eg groom outside, keep doors and windows open when handling hay or straw inside. Soaking hay and using 'clean' bedding or proprietary made 'dust free' bedding all helps to reduce the concentrations of dust and spores. If exposure is for long periods, eg when stacking straw during delivery, wear a suitable dust respirator that complies with BS 2091:1969 (with a type B filter) or with BS 6016 Type 2, or with a harmonised European standard.

Zoonoses

64 Zoonoses are diseases which can be transmitted from animals to humans. Ringworm and leptospirosis (Weil's disease) are two such diseases and steps should be taken to protect employees.

Ringworm

65 Ringworm is primarily associated with cattle although other animals are infective, eg horses, pigs, sheep, vermin. The spores are normally transmitted by direct skin to skin contact; contact with infected surfaces, such as fence rails, provides a more minor source. Animal faeces may also transmit viable spores. Spores enter the skin through abrasions, cuts or puncture wounds. Spores can remain viable outdoors for several months and indoors for up to five years. Ringworm starts as a small inflamed and swollen area which rapidly progresses to a round, white, crusty lesion. It is normally found on areas where direct contact has occurred, eg hands, forearms, head, and neck. 'Rings' may appear resulting in large patches, often with associated hair loss. Sometimes swellings, resembling boils, occur especially on the jaws.

66 Infected animals should be treated and steps should be taken to prevent the spread of the disease. Protective clothing, ie rubber gloves, washable overall/apron and rubber boots should be worn when handling infected animals. The clothing should be thoroughly washed after use and treated with a suitable fungicide. All cuts should be kept clean and covered with a waterproof dressing. The hands, forearms, face and neck should be washed after work.

Leptospirosis (Weil's Disease)

67 This is a serious and sometimes fatal infection that is transmitted to humans by contact with urine from infected rats. Other forms of the disease are associated with cattle urine. The bacteria can enter the body through cuts and abrasions and through the lining of the mouth, throat and eyes after contact with infected urine or contaminated water such as in ditches, ponds and slow flowing rivers. Rat urine may also contaminate animal feed and bedding. The symptoms are a flu-like illness with a persistent and severe headache. In severe cases the kidneys may be damaged and jaundice develops.

68 To protect employees from leptospirosis a strict pest control system must be employed to eradicate rats. All cuts and broken skin should be covered by waterproof plasters. Hands should be washed after handling any animal or possible contaminated material, for example bales of straw, and always before eating, drinking or smoking. Suspect illnesses should be reported to a doctor promptly. In some occupations employees carry cards to alert their GP to the nature of their work to aid diagnosis. The card which is free, can be obtained from the HSE Information Centre (see Appendix 7). Further advice can be obtained from your doctor or the Employment Medical Advisory Service at the local Health and Safety Executive office. The number can be found in the phone book.

Other risks to workers

Tetanus

69 Although it is not zoonotic, tetanus can be passed from horses to people. The tetanus bacillus lives in the intestine of horses and soil contaminated with droppings. Manure heaps provide a good growth medium for the organism. The organism enters the human body usually through a cut, abrasion or penetrating injury. This could be from a bite by an infected horse or being stabbed in the foot by a contaminated pitch fork. Often the workers do not notice minor wounds and leave them untreated and uncovered.

70 People affected suffer from severe muscle contractions, usually in the neck but also in the body. The disease is very painful and may end in death.

71 It is essential that everyone in contact with horses should be vaccinated against tetanus. Information should also be given on the types of injury likely to give rise to tetanus and how to deal with such an injury, eg seeking medical attention. All cuts and broken skin should be kept covered by a waterproof dressing.

Pesticides

72 The Control of Pesticides Regulations 1986 covers the storage and use of pesticides such as fungicides, herbicides, insecticides, public hygiene pest control products, rodenticides and wood preservatives. Everyone who uses pesticides should be competent in the tasks undertaken and should have received adequate information and training to use pesticides safely and legally. If pesticides approved for agricultural use are used the operator may require a Certificate of Competence. Only approved pesticides should be used. The instructions on the label should be rigidly adhered to. Where labels have faded and are unreadable, the pesticide should be disposed of in a safe, approved way. Local waste

Figure 2 *Cautionary warning sign (black with yellow background)*

regulation authorities can give advice on disposal, including details of facilities available locally. The waste regulation authorities are county councils (for non-metropolitan areas) and district councils or single purpose waste authorities (for metropolitan areas) in England, district councils in Wales and district or island councils in Scotland.

73 All pesticides should be stored in a suitably constructed, secure bin, cabinet, chest or vault capable of resisting fire for at least 30 minutes and robust enough to withstand reasonably foreseeable accidental impact. The store needs to be fitted with a sump which will retain the total capacity of the contents stored, in the event of all containers failing simultaneously (eg in the case of a fire). It should not be sited within a staff room, office, or any areas used for storing or preparing animal feed and if kept outside then it needs to be waterproof. The pesticide store should be identified by a cautionary warning sign (see Figure 2) and smoking prohibited in the area. For large quantities of pesticides, containers specifically manufactured to comply with the legislative requirements for storage are available on the market. Otherwise, a purpose-built pesticide store should be constructed.

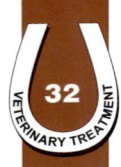

VETERINARY TREATMENT

74 All veterinary drugs and medicines should be kept in a designated, secure (eg locked) cabinet, chest or cupboard to prevent access by children, other unauthorised persons, animals, birds and vermin. The medicines should be stored in accordance with the recommendations on the label/data sheet or the veterinary surgeon's instructions to ensure they meet their stated shelf lives. Unsuitable storage conditions may lead to veterinary medicines becoming contaminated, spoiled by vermin or otherwise becoming ineffective, eg some veterinary medicines can be damaged by exposure to light.

75 All people who handle and/or administer veterinary medicines should be given adequate information, instruction and training and be competent. Information should also be given on the potential dangers of the veterinary medicines being inadvertently administered to those attending the horse, eg some may be fatal to humans in the dose administered to the horse. Employers and the self-employed should ensure that the procedures identified in the COSHH assessment are followed; only the minimum quantity of veterinary medicines necessary for treatment is removed from the store; the horse is kept calm and is securely restrained while the veterinary medicine is administered (see paragraph 80 for restraining methods).

76 All syringes and needles should be disposed of using a 'sharps bin'. Proprietary sharps bins can be obtained from suppliers of animal health products. Used needles should not be disposed of in domestic waste. On no account should soft drink cans, plastic bottles or similar containers be used for the disposal of needles, since these could present serious hazards to staff if they were to be disposed of in domestic waste.

77 Veterinarians may use their own portable X-ray equipment at riding establishments. The operator of this equipment will be responsible for ensuring its safe use, but employers should be aware of the dangers and ensure that only nominated staff who have been fully instructed and protected are permitted to assist in radiography

work. The Ionising Radiations Regulations 1985 apply to the use of this type of equipment. It is recommended that veterinarians or farriers are assisted only by fully trained and experienced people. Simple treatment may normally be undertaken within the horse's own stable. Complex treatment should only be administered if the horse is adequately restrained.

Disposal of medicines

78 All outdated or unwanted veterinary medicines should be disposed of safely. Prior to disposal all wastes should be stored safely and securely. Local waste regulation authorities can give advice on disposal, including details of facilities available locally.

79 Further information on veterinary medicines is given in the booklet *Veterinary medicines: Safe use by farmers and other animal handlers*[8].

Restraining the horse

80 The horse should be handled quietly but firmly by an experienced person. A bridle rather than a head collar may be necessary for horses where extra control is needed, or where the horse is known to be difficult. Some possible methods of restraint are:

(a) holding up the horse's front leg;

(b) grasping the horse's tail and pulling it firmly downwards when treating or attending to the hindquarters;

(c) holding a fold of skin on the neck;

(d) using a twitch on the upper lip of the muzzle.

It is important not to be over-aggressive as this will upset the horse. Using the minimum amount of force and keeping the horse calm will help to diffuse a potentially hazardous situation. The handler should wear strong or safety footwear, gloves and protective headgear. Treatment given in a quiet, secure area, away from distractions, will help to calm the horse.

ENVIRONMENT AND WELFARE

81 The Workplace (Health, Safety and Welfare) Regulations 1992[9] aim to ensure that workplaces meet the health, safety and welfare needs of each member of the workforce. Premises built after 1 January 1993, or existing premises modified, extended or converted after that date will have to comply with the Regulations. All other premises will be required to comply from 1 January 1996. These Regulations give more detail to the general duties of employers under the Health and Safety at Work etc Act 1974.

Stabling

82 The construction of stables is dealt with under the Riding Establishment Acts 1964 and 1970. However, under health and safety legislation, riding establishments will need to consider whether the size and construction of the stable is adequate and provides a safe place of work. Lack of space can contribute to handlers being squashed or trodden on when attending to the horse.

Ventilation

83 It is important that the stables are well ventilated. Stables tend to be dusty and have fumes from urine and faeces which pose a potential hazard to the handlers if good ventilation is not provided. Stables with high pitched roofs generally have good air circulation. Windows hinged at the bottom with the sides blocked will allow air flow up and around the stable and provide extra ventilation. Windows should be either protected by metal bars or made of plate or wired glass.

Floors

84 Stable floors soundly constructed, slip-resistant to both horse and handler and impervious to moisture will help to prevent slips, trips and falls. Concrete slabs with a grooved surface are slip resistant and assist with drainage. Smooth concrete becomes slippery when wet and may need to be treated or replaced to reduce the risks of slipping.

Figure 3 *Stable doors*

Internal walls and partitions

85 Walls and partitions of strong construction, solid and free of nails and other protrusions will help to prevent injury to horse and handler. A ring placed about head height should be provided for the horse.

Doors

86 Stable doors in two halves, so that the upper portion can be left open, will allow anyone entering the stable to see where the horse is and its condition before opening the lower half. If a horse is known to bite, a grille should be placed over the top opening to prevent it

biting anyone who approaches the stable. The horse may injure itself by banging its hip joints or legs and also trap the handler between the door frame and itself, if the doors are too narrow. Doors which open outwards allow quick access to be gained to an injured person lying behind the door or to sick horses. A horse can easily push through a flimsy or damaged door. Doors of substantial construction fitted with two heavy-duty hinges on each door with bolts at the top and bottom, will help to prevent this (see Figure 3).

Lighting

87 All electric wiring and light bulbs should be protected. Light switches should be outside the stable and never within reach of a horse. They should be specifically designed for external use. The main control should be in a secure area so that lighting cannot be switched off inadvertently.

Access to haylofts

88 A properly constructed staircase which is provided with handrails is the preferred means of access to haylofts. Where ladders are used, it is important that they:

(a) are maintained in good condition, of sound construction with no defects and in particular the rungs of any wooden ladder should not be solely supported by nails or screws;

(b) supported on a firm, level surface;

(c) securely fixed to the structure so that it cannot slip, with lashings, straps or proprietary clips;

(d) extended to a height of at least 1.05 m above the landing place or above the highest rung on which the user has to stand unless there is an equivalent suitable handhold;

(e) placed at a suitable angle to minimise the risk of slipping (ideally at about 75° to the horizontal, ie about 1 m out from the building for every 4 m in height).

Collecting yard

89 Riders should mount horses in a safe area, which is level, has a slip-resistant surface and is kept free from obstruction.

Riding areas or manege

90 Riding areas enclosed by fencing will help to provide a secure area where both horse and rider can be easily managed. The fencing should ideally be post and rail with the rails facing inwards and high enough to prevent the horses from jumping over. Gates wide enough to allow the horse to pass through will prevent damage to the animal. A safe riding area will be well drained, free from rabbit holes, mole hills and other obstructions. Glass and litter should be removed immediately. If the riding area is floodlit, the cables should be protected from horse, rider and traffic. Show jumps and any other equipment used should be soundly constructed with no sharp edges or protrusions, and cleared from the riding area when not in use. The removal of jump cups from the wings when not required, will help to support jumping poles.

Figure 4 *Kicking boards*

Indoor schools

91 Ideally, doors into the indoor school should be of a sliding type or open outwards and be provided with kicking boards. It is advised that kicking boards, no less than 1.35 m (4 feet 6 inches) high should be fixed to the internal walls and slope outwards at an angle of around 10°(see Figure 4). The school should be well lit with the lights set at a height which will not interfere with the horse and rider. There should be no obstructions or protrusions. Displaying a sign giving instructions on entering, leaving and use of the school will help to ensure that everyone is aware of the correct procedures. Providing training for both the horse and rider on how to enter the school steadily will help to prevent accidents occurring from horses rushing in and out of the school.

Grazing paddocks

92 Saddles and bridles should be used when horses are ridden into the paddocks. Instructions and training should be given on how to release and catch a horse safely in the paddock without being kicked. If the horse's head is held towards the handler and made to face the gate while the head collar is removed, the handler is less likely to be kicked by an excitable horse. If grazing paddocks are used as riding areas then paragraph 90 will be helpful.

Visitors' areas

93 Where possible, car parks should be situated away from the riding area, and, where appropriate, speed limits imposed. A traffic flow system which takes account of pedestrian movements and minimises reversing will reduce the risk of an accident. Viewing areas that are clearly defined and well lit will allow visitors to watch others riding without being exposed to danger. Visitors should not be allowed to interfere with those riding. Small children should be carefully supervised as they often show no fear with horses and do not appreciate the dangers of being near to horses.

General horse handling

Loading and unloading facilities

94 Safe loading and unloading of horses in transport will include loading and unloading in a calm manner, particularly where horses have not previously been transported and using anti-slip loading ramps, which are not steeply inclined. Attendants should not stand directly beneath the ramp when lowering or raising it.

Handling in restricted areas

95 If a horse has to be moved in a restricted area or near obstructions which pose a risk either to the horse or the handler, the horse should always be led.

Lungeing manege

96 Lungeing should only be carried out in a defined fenced manege by competent people. Only those authorised or undergoing instruction should be permitted within the area during lungeing.

General housekeeping

97 Many accidents result from trips and falls which may be prevented by good housekeeping. Accidents can be avoided if the means of access to the riding school and any passages, paths or roads and any part of the premises to which employees or visitors have access are kept clear of obstruction and have surfaces which minimise the risk of slipping. Pot holes, broken steps, stairs or treads, uneven paving, holes in stable floors, defective gates and door fastenings, broken gates and doors, projections of wood or metal in unexpected places, passages blocked by barrels, buckets, bales of hay or straw, and forks or shovels lying about in or by any access ways are all potential hazards to visitors and employees at the premises. Good housekeeping prevents accidents occurring.

Children

98 Extra care is necessary to ensure that children are not put at risk from work activities. Horses, machinery, buildings and chemicals can present particular risks to children and young people unless adequate precautions are taken. Falls and falling objects, as well as drowning in grain, slurry and water, have continued to cause unnecessary death or injury.

Facilities for employees

99 If people are employed to work in riding establishments the Workplace (Health, Safety and Welfare) Regulations 1992[6] will apply. The nature of riding establishment work means that employees may spend much of their time working outdoors. Basic facilities for washing, getting warm and sanitary conveniences should be provided. Keeping warm during the cold weather is not always easy. Workers are particularly at risk from cold when the temperature around them is below 10°C. Where the air temperature is 10°C and the wind speed is 20 miles per hour, the effective temperature, so far as the body is concerned, drops to 0°C. During cold and/or wet weather employees should be allowed rest periods in a warm area with facilities for making hot drinks and drying clothes. In the case of new workplaces in operation from 1 January 1993, a separate rest room should be provided. For existing workplaces a rest area is sufficient. Rest areas and rest rooms should be large enough, and have sufficient chairs and tables, for the number of employees likely to use them at any one time. Arrangements should be made to protect non-smokers from discomfort caused by tobacco smoke.

Toilet and washing facilities

Table 1

1 Number of people at work	2 Number of water closets	3 Number of washing stations
1 - 5	1	1
6 - 25	2	2
26 - 50	3	3
51 - 75	4	4
76 -100	5	5

100 Sanitary facilities should be under cover, partitioned off for privacy, have adequate lighting, ventilation and proper doors and fastenings. Where female facilities are provided, suitable means for disposal of sanitary dressings should be available. Wash hand basins should be provided with a continuous supply of hot and cold water, soap and drying facilities such as towels, paper towels or hot air driers. Where facilities provided for workers are also used by members of the public, this should not prejudice the workers' use of the facilities. The numbers of sanitary conveniences and washing facilities should be increased if necessary.

Information for employees

101 The Health and Safety (Information for Employees) Regulations 1989 requires that certain information is given to employees. The necessary information is provided on the poster *Health and safety law - what you should know*. The poster should be displayed in a location where employees will see it. Alternatively leaflets containing the same information as the poster may be given to each employee. The poster may be purchased and leaflets can be obtained free of charge from HSE Books (see back cover for details).

TACK

102 Rider safety and control of the horse may be seriously impaired unless all tack is in good condition and checked before use to ensure it is free from defects. Particular attention should be paid to the stitching, as the life of the thread is short compared to that of the leather. Horse sweat rots the stitching and leather, so all tack should be kept clean and supple and be well maintained. It is important that the tack is suitable and comfortable to both the horse and the rider. Each horse should have its own correctly fitted tack which is suitable for the activity to be carried out.

The saddle

103 If properly looked after and kept well maintained, saddles will last for many years (see Figure 5). Regular safety checks should be carried out on the saddle, these will include the following:

(a) *The girth straps and their attachment* (see Figure 6). Girth straps are stitched onto webs which pass over the saddle tree. The stitching will eventually perish and will need to be replaced. Girth straps also become worn, usually stretched and split around the holes. When this occurs the strap should be replaced. Saddles which have girth straps attached to the tree by tacks are often insecure and should be avoided.

(b) *The stirrup bar safety catch*. This should always be in the open or down position when the saddle is being used. This allows the stirrup leather to be freed from the saddle in the event of a fall, preventing the rider from being dragged.

Stirrup leathers

104 Stirrup leathers should be inspected thoroughly before use (see Figure 7), for the thickness of the leather in relation to the stirrup bar, the stitching on the buckle end and around the holes. Any stirrup leather found to be less than satisfactory, ie with cracked,

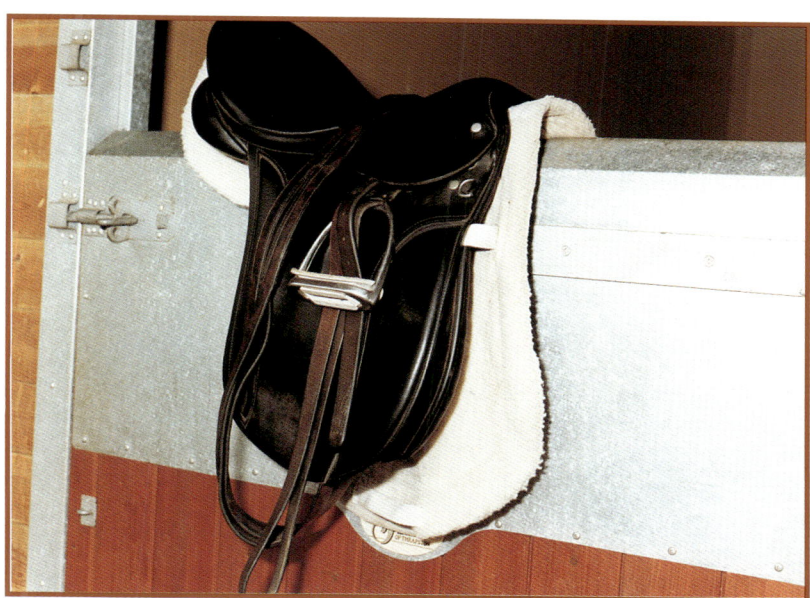

Figure 5 *Saddle*

Figure 6 *Girth straps*

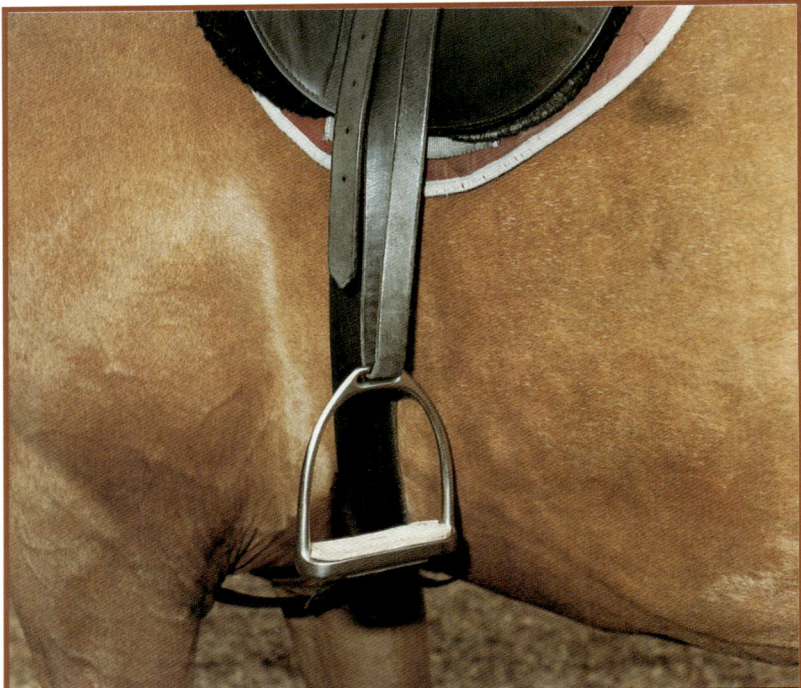

Figure 7 *Srirrup leathers and irons*

worn leather or rotten stitching should not be used. Stirrup leathers which are too long for the rider should have extra holes punched in them and not be wound around the stirrup iron to make them shorter.

Stirrup irons

105 High quality stirrup irons such as stainless steel are less likely to snap or become deformed. It is important that the stirrup iron is of the correct size for the rider, so that it slips off the foot easily in an emergency but is not too big, allowing the whole foot to slip through and become trapped. Consider using safety irons which are available for children and novice riders. All the safety stirrups incorporate a design or device which allows the foot to be released in an emergency.

Figure 8 Bridle and bit.

Bridles

106 Bridles should be of good quality. The stitching should be regularly inspected, along with the buckles and hook studs. Buckles should not be sharp so as to cut into the leather or have bent or loose tongues (see Figure 8). Bent or loose hook studs should be replaced. Rein stops should be used on the reins when using a running martingale. This prevents the rings of the martingale becoming fast on the buckles or hook studs on the reins near the bit and impairing the rider's control over the horse.

Bits

107 High quality bits such as those made from stainless steel are less likely to snap and become deformed.

RIDING AND ROAD SAFETY

Rider safety

108 Instructors should ensure that the horse or pony provided for a rider's use (employee, trainee or client) is suitable and safe for that person, taking into account age, size, experience, general riding ability and any known handicap or limitation of the rider. Riders should be given information about the horse's character and behaviour. Novice riders should be given a quiet, steady horse or pony and the instructor to student ratio adjusted accordingly. The lesson should be held in a small, secure manege. On no account should novice riders be allowed to ride on the road unless led or accompanied by an experienced, competent person.

Personal protective equipment (PPE)

109 The Personal Protective Equipment at Work Regulations 1992[10] require that suitable personal protective equipment should be used by employees wherever there is a risk to health and safety that cannot be adequately controlled by other means. This includes, eg the provision of safety footwear where there is a risk of foot injuries, headgear where there is a risk of head injuries or suitable outdoor clothing if the job involves working outside in adverse weather conditions.

Protective headgear

110 The high number of head injuries, often of a severe nature, which occur make wearing protective headgear a necessary measure. Riders, as well as handlers who may be exposed to head injuries, should wear suitable protective headgear, correctly adjusted and fitted. Protective headgear considered to be suitable is that conforming to BS 6473: 1984[11] or BS 4472: 1988[12]. Additionally, cycle helmets conforming to BS 6863: 1989[13] are listed as approved headgear in the Horses (Protective Headgear for Young Riders) Regulations 1992 which make it mandatory for children under the age of 14 to wear protective headgear when riding horses on the *road*.

Figure 9 Protective headgear

Appropriate headgear conforming to the PPE (EC Directive) Regulations 1992 (implementing the PPE Product Directive which requires PPE to be 'CE' marked) will also be considered suitable (Figure 9 illustrates two types of protective headgear).

111 It is important to check that headgear is correctly worn and adjusted. New riders may need to be shown how to carry out adjustments.

112 Protective headgear should be replaced periodically according to use and manufacturers' recommendations. Damaged or dropped hats should not be worn until checked for safe use by the manufacturer or other competent person.

Rider dress

113 The traditional riding dress is very expensive, therefore it is unreasonable to expect casual riders or those new to the sport to have purchased the necessary clothing. Certain items of riding equipment such as safety footwear and protective headgear to the current BSI Standard(s) (see paragraph 110) should be worn.

Footwear

114 Riding boots are preferred but suitable alternatives may be allowed for, eg stout, strong shoes with a good heel up to one inch (2.5 cm) to prevent the foot from slipping through the stirrup iron. Riders should not be allowed to wear plimsolls or trainers, wellingtons or sandals, unless suitable and safe adaptions to the tack have been made. Sensible (ie strong and slip-resistant) footwear is not only essential for riding but safety footwear should be worn when handling horses and mucking out to protect the feet from trampling and prevent possible puncture wounds by the fork.

Handlers' dress

115 Gloves can help to prevent friction burns to the hands when leading horses with a rope.

Other clothing

116 It is recommended that arms and shoulders are covered to avoid the risk of abrasions during a fall, even in the warmest weather. Jackets which are fastened so that they cannot flap about will help to prevent distractions to the horse or rider. Tight clothing may restrict free movement of the body. Long hair which is tied back or secured with a hair net will help with visibility. It is advisable that jewellery, in particular rings and earrings, should not be worn. Rings may become caught in the horse's mane and cause cuts to the fingers, while earrings can become tangled in hair nets and may rip the ear lobe. Alternatively, gloves may afford protection against rings becoming caught.

Road safety

117 Every year there are many road accidents involving horses and motor vehicles, some organisations report as many as eight every day. Generally, horses and motor vehicles should be kept apart. Horses are easily frightened by noisy, large vehicles and other events not normally encountered in a stable or field, eg a person mowing the lawn, children playing football. Motorists often do not appreciate the behaviour of horses and will drive too quickly and too closely to the horse. However, there are occasions when horses have to go onto the roads to gain access to bridle paths or when training either horse or rider. Only horses that are trained in traffic should be allowed on the road, especially if being ridden by an inexperienced rider.

Figure 10

118 Groups should be kept small, no more than five or six, and organised so that:

(a) the least experienced riders are on the quietest horses;

(b) riders with least experience are in the middle of the ride;

(c) young or nervous horses are positioned on the inside of an older experienced horse but under no circumstances should riders ride more than two abreast;

(d) experienced riders are always at the front and rear of the ride. The majority of road surfaces are very slippery and therefore it is recommended that the ride be conducted at a walking pace. Never canter on grass verges at the side of roads.

119 It is important that the riders are clearly visible to motorists. Fluorescent and reflective tabards and armbands are available for riders and legbands for the horses (see Figure 12).

Figure 11

Figure 12 *Fluorescent and reflective tabards and arm bands for rider. Fluorescent and reflective legbands for horse.*

120 Employees should have received sufficient and adequate information, instruction and training to allow them to ride safely on roads without putting themselves or others at risk.

121 The British Horse Society run courses and Road Safety Certificates, often in conjunction with the local authority road safety officer. All aspects of road safety are covered, including the Highway Code, control of the horse, tack safety checks, horse foot care and shoeing, accident procedures, first aid and riding in the dark.

122 It is recommended that, ideally, employees should hold the British Horse Society Road Riding Escort Certificate or have received equivalent training (training records should be kept) before being allowed to accompany clients on the road. They should, at least, hold the Riding and Road Safety Certificate. In some areas the Association of British Riding Schools, in conjunction with the Police, operate similar safety certificates. Further information can be obtained from the British Horse Society or the Association of British Riding Schools (see Appendix 7).

Leading a horse on the highway

123 Movement of horses across or along the public highway should always be undertaken in a prescribed safe manner and riders should be supervised and trained to adhere to safety procedures for horses as specified in the Highway Code.

124 Horses led either on foot or from another horse should be on the left-hand side of the road and led from the handler's left, placing the handler between the horse and the traffic.

125 A bridle should be worn when leading a horse on the highway and whenever leading a saddled horse, the stirrups should be 'run up' and secured.

ELECTRICAL SAFETY

126 The use of electricity at riding establishment premises is subject to the Electricity at Work Regulations 1989. The Regulations require employers and self-employed people to maintain, so far as is reasonably practicable, electrical systems and electrical equipment within their control. Electricity can cause shock, burns and start fires. It should therefore never be treated lightly. Electrical equipment within work premises should be installed and maintained by a competent person. If using an outside contractor, one way of demonstrating competence would be to select an organisation who is certificate holder of the National Inspection Council for Electrical Installation Contracting (NICEIC).

Fixed electrical installations

127 All fixed electrical installations should be designed, installed, operated and maintained to prevent electrical danger. The Institution of Electrical Engineers produces guidance on testing and inspection of fixed installations. This is now in its sixteenth edition and is called the *Regulations for Electrical Installations*[14]. This is recognised as a British Standard (BS 7671:1992). It should be remembered that despite its title, these are *not* a legal requirement.

128 The IEE recommend that fixed electrical installations should be inspected and tested at regular intervals and for horse riding establishments this would normally be at least once every three years. This should be done by a competent person who should advise of any defects and prepare a report indicating such defects. All defects considered serious by the competent person should be remedied as soon as possible after being reported. The possession of such a report is one way of demonstrating compliance with the Electricity at Work Regulations 1989, in respect of maintenance of the installation.

Electrical equipment

129 Providing sufficient 13 amp socket outlets fitted with switches will reduce the need for multi-adaptors and trailing cables. Sockets sited away from the reach of horses will prevent them seizing cables and plugs with their teeth when the sockets are in use. Socket outlets and switches sited outdoors should be appropriate for that use, ie be of weatherproof construction. Domestic 13 amp plugs and sockets are not suitable for use in wet or dirty conditions. BS 1363 fittings are suitable when marked with IP 43 or IP 44. Where there is a harmonised European standard, this would also be suitable.

130 Where it is unavoidable to have a trailing cable, this should be adequately protected from mechanical damage and should not cause a tripping hazard. Damaged cables should generally be replaced completely. Never carry out makeshift repairs to cables. When joining flexible cables, proper connectors should be used, ie not chocolate block connectors.

131 Suitable and properly maintained residual current devices (RCDs) should be installed where clippers, grooming machines and pressure washers are used. In addition, all electrical equipment used outdoors should be controlled by a RCD. Fixed devices should comply with BS 4293: 1983. Portable devices should comply with BS 7071: 1989. Where there is a harmonised European standard this would also be appropriate. The test button on the RCD should be operated on a monthly basis to ensure the continued effective operation of the device.

132 Where practicable, hand held equipment should be at a reduced voltage, 110 volts from a centre tapped to earth transformer and provided with a non-detachable, flexible cable incorporating an earth continuity conductor for connecting to the earthing contact or terminal of the appliance. The latter requirement does not apply to double insulated equipment. Extra low voltage equipment, such as clippers, are available, and preference should be given to these. The risk of fatal injury from electric shock is greater from the use of hand held electrical equipment than for other types of portable apparatus

under similar conditions because the hand is usually already tightly gripping the equipment, making it difficult or impossible for the victim to let go. If the earth continuity conductor is broken, the operator provides the only path to earth in the event of an electrical fault.

133 Regular in-house visual checks should be carried out on all electrical equipment by a designated member of staff to ensure cables are in good condition, plugs are correctly attached and the equipment is in general good repair. These checks can be undertaken by the user before and during use. Staff who have received training may be able to check fuse ratings or earth connections. However, no-one should carry out electrical work unless they have sufficient knowledge to prevent a danger to themselves or others. The equipment should be maintained and serviced as recommended by the manufacturers. Any equipment that is found to be defective or unsuitable for use during initial or routine inspections should be withdrawn from service. In addition to the routine electrical checks, some equipment may need to be tested by a competent electrician. For example, a visual check may not pick up an internal fault. The Regulations do not specify any frequencies for such tests, simply that the equipment should be maintained to prevent the likelihood of danger arising. It is clearly sensible to keep records of all the inspections and tests carried out on each piece of equipment.

134 Clipping and electrical grooming should be carried out by a competent person in a dry stable with the bedding and water buckets removed. An additional person assisting who is capable of handling the horse will help if it becomes difficult or nervous. Cleaning the appliances after use will prevent them becoming clogged with hair, grease and dust from the horse's coat.

135 Practical guidance on electricity is given in some detail in several publications[14-18].

MACHINERY

136 All machinery and its safeguards should be kept in good condition and be regularly serviced in accordance with the manufacturer's instructions. In general, machinery should only be used for the task for which it was designed. Sometimes accidents have occurred when machinery has been misused. Any person using a machine should be given appropriate information, instruction and training on how to use the machine and on the hazards or risks associated with its use. When not in use, machinery should be disconnected or isolated from its power supply to protect against unauthorised use and to reduce the potential for accidents.

Approaching dangerous parts - power isolation

137 When access to the dangerous parts of any of the above machines is needed for maintenance, cleaning, adjustment and blockage removal, the machine should be isolated from the power, ie switched off by means of an isolating switch or unplugged at the mains. For power take-off (PTO) driven machines, the tractor power should be disconnected and the PTO disengaged.

Tractors

138 Routine checks will help to ensure that:

(a) brakes on tractors and equipment are connected and working efficiently;

(b) steering is maintained so that there is no excessive free movement and no unnecessary play on the front wheel bearings;

(c) tyres are inflated to the correct pressure and have adequate tread. They should not be used if they have suffered damage which could affect their safe use.

139 Tractors can overturn in certain situations such as on sloping fields, hills etc, or when driven recklessly. Providing tractors with an approved cab, frame or roll bar, will give the driver protection in the event of overturning. Some tractors may have exemption certificates to allow entry into low buildings.

140 Drivers should be adequately trained, particularly to recognise potentially dangerous situations. The training should emphasise the need for care and concentration when working with tractors and, in particular, the importance of paying attention to changes in ground conditions which may affect the safety of the operation.

141 A tractor PTO and the power take-off shaft of a machine can be extremely dangerous and normally require guarding. Some equipment, however, is designed in such a way that there is no access to rotating points. Every year operators are killed or seriously injured in accidents involving PTO and PTO shafts.

142 Many of these accidents would have been prevented if the PTO and PTO shaft had been correctly fitted with guards which were properly used and maintained.

143 The tractor PTO should be protected by a shield covering the top and both sides of the PTO so that people and their clothes are protected from contact with it. This shield should be substantially constructed and be capable of supporting at least 120 kg. When the PTO is not in use it may be covered by a fixed cap and the shield is not then required.

144 PTO shafts should be totally enclosed by the guard. The shaft should be guarded along its whole length from the tractor to the first bearing on the machine. BS 3417, Parts 1, 2 and 3 (or where there is a harmonised European standard) give details of guarding requirements, and strength and wear tests.

145 Certain components on tractors can be a hazard and need guarding, eg engine fan, dynamo pulley, fan belt run on points and the fuel injection coupling drive. The tractor should have a suitable

mounting and dismounting step fitted not more than 550 mm from the ground. All hydraulic controls need marking to show the effect of movement and the tractor should have a positive stopping device identified with the method of operation.

Grass cutters

146 In addition to the guarding of the cutting discs or blades and moving parts, the grass cutter should normally be provided with a skirt that reaches to the ground. Fatalities have occurred when stones have been thrown out by the machine, hitting people nearby. Accidents have also arisen when the blades and attachments of rotary mowers are not properly maintained or fixed in a position and fly loose. Blades and cutting discs should be replaced if they become damaged or worn to the extent that safety may be compromised.

Chaff cutters

147 Guards are required to prevent access to the blades. The guards should prevent the blades from being reached through either the inlet or outlet of the machine. In addition, care should be taken when feeding in the material.

Oat rollers

148 The in-running nip, ie the direction of the roller movement, causes clothing and fingers to be dragged into the machine. A guard should be fitted preventing access to the rollers. Accidents have occurred when hands have been placed up the discharge outlet and come into contact with the moving components. On older machines the discharge outlet chute should be lengthened or fitted with a suitable guard to prevent access.

Horse walkers

149 Horse walkers should be installed in an area where contact with unauthorised people is unlikely to occur. People not directly handling the horses should be kept out of the area.

Steam/water pressure cleaners

150 Steam/water pressure cleaners are often used for washing down vehicles, buildings, and yards. On average 2-3 people die each year from electrocution and many more receive burns or shocks from these machines. Most injuries occur when the metal lance at the end of the flexible hose becomes live through an electrical fault. Electrical faults are caused by:

(a) an unsafe or inadequate electric extension cable;

(b) the wrong type of power cable connector, especially one that is not watertight;

(c) damage to the power cable by running the cleaner over it, by another vehicle running over it or by heat from the machine;

(d) a loose earth wire inside the plug.

An electric shock from one of these machines is likely to be made more severe by the wet conditions that surround the machine and operator. The machine should be used with a circulating current earth monitoring device or a residual current device. These devices should be fitted at the mains supply point, where they should be protected from splash by a waterproof cover. Further advice is contained in the Guidance Note PM 29 *Electrical hazards from steam/water pressure cleaners etc*[19].

APPENDIX 1: HORSE BEHAVIOUR

1   The evolution of the horse has taken place over millions of years and the modern horse is gregarious and a herbivore. Wild horses form herds and each herd has a dominant stallion. Horses kept in fields will also have a leader and lower rankings.

2   The horse is not naturally aggressive to people and will normally run away when frightened. However, it will fight to establish a social hierarchy, protect its young, secure food, and defend itself if it feels threatened and cannot escape.

3   In order to handle horses safely the instincts and senses of the horse must be considered. Accidents can easily be caused by a handler (or a visitor to the premises) upsetting or frightening the horse.

Figure 13   *The correct approach to a horse*

Senses

4   The horse has the same five senses as human beings:

(a) *Sight.* The horse is a non-predator and is thought to have relatively poor sight. A horse which appears to be looking into the distance may actually be using other more developed senses. Unlike humans, the horse is able to see images to the left and right at the same time due to the eyes being at the side of the head. A horse should always be approached from the side and not from its blind spot, that is directly in front, or behind, as this could startle it (see Figure 13).

(b) *Smell.* Smell is a very important sense to the horse and is used to detect good from bad. If a horse is confused it will sniff the air. It should be noted that some perfumes have a musk base which could excite a horse, particularly stallions. Therefore perfumes should not be worn, and scented soaps and body sprays should be avoided when working with stallions.

(c) *Hearing.* The horse has large mobile ears and acute hearing. Often it can hear something well before it sees the object or before humans hear the same noise, if humans are able to hear the noise at all. By turning its ears towards the sound, a horse is able to accurately determine the direction from which it is coming.

(d) *Touch.* The sensory nerves throughout the body are more pronounced in areas devoid of hair or with little skeletal frame such as the ears and muzzle. Pressure is often exerted on these areas by handlers when attempting to restrain difficult horses.

(e) *Taste.* This is the least used of the senses and is insignificant as an indicator of horse behaviour.

The frightened horse

In the field

5 The horse will throw its head up and prick its ears. It will tense the muscles from the muzzle to the tail, open the nostrils to smell and fill its lungs with oxygen ready for flight. In a field, the horse will only attack when cornered. Horses which bolt when frightened often knock people down or run into things because the horse is looking behind at whatever frightened it, rather than where its going. This is known as 'blind fright'.

In the stable

6 The horse when frightened will initially still try to run away but because it is cornered will then revert to its survival instincts. It will usually give a warning before biting or kicking by swinging its rear end, swishing its tail and flicking its ears. If the warning is ignored, it will tense from muzzle to tail, clench the tail between its rear legs and kick or lay its ears flat back with the eyes standing proud, curl the mouth and lunge forward with the neck straight, ready to bite. It is important that everyone involved in handling horses can recognise the warning signs for their own well-being. Horses known to be temperamental should only be handled by experienced staff and have a warning sign on their stable doors.

Causes of fear

7 Any sudden movement, sudden noise or any unusual event or occurrence can frighten horses and ponies. Horses do not have reasoning power and are creatures of habit. If a horse has become used to an environment it may react in an unforeseen way, even when there is no obvious danger in the reasoned opinion of a human, eg the presence of a new road sign could result in a horse refusing to follow a previously established route.

APPENDIX 2: SELF-AUDIT CHECK-LIST

The following check-list may be used to help direct your attention to areas in the establishment which require regular examination. It is by no means an exhaustive list and should be adapted to suit your particular establishment

1. Records up to date eg
   - machinery maintained
   - equipment maintained
   - accident/incident
   - COSHH assessment
   - staff training
   - pesticides in stock
   - inspection of fire extinguishers

2. Procedures
   - need updating
   - review of safety policy
   - management policies
   - emergency procedures (doctor's name/ telephone number)

3. Staff training
   - new staff
   - new equipment
   - new procedures

4. First-aid kit
   - fully stocked

5. COSHH
   - assessment up to date
   - new products/tasks added
   - new staff informed

6   Drugs and pesticides
        - cupboard locked

7   Electrical safety
        - appliances in good condition
        - appliances have correct fuse
        - sufficient sockets
        - plugs, sockets and fittings in good condition and working order

8   Machinery
        - guards correctly fitted
        - machine in good condition
        - used only by competent persons

9   Manual handling
        - good techniques used
        - lifting aids used
        - bales stacked safely

10 Premises general
        - stables in sound condition
        - fencing in good condition
        - floors non-slip
        - no obstructions
        - adequate lighting/ventilation
        - visitors areas separate to riding areas
        - safe access to lofts

11 Tack
        - stitching in good condition
        - straps not worn
        - fits horse

12 Protective clothing
        - British Standard hats used
        - suitable footwear worn
        - suitable clothing

APPENDIX 3: ADVICE ON SAFETY POLICY STATEMENTS

1 Written safety policy statements are only required if there are five or more employees. The statement may be considered as being in three parts:

(a) the statement of the employers' general policy with regard to the health and safety of their employees;

(b) the organisation for carrying out the policy;

(c) the arrangements for carrying out the policy.

2 The statement should cover the intent to comply with current statutory provisions and should lay particular emphasis on safe work routines. It should stress the importance of co-operation from the workforce and of good communications at all levels in the business. The statement should be signed by the employer or a partner or senior director.

3 Where necessary, the statement should clearly define the responsibilities of named senior and junior members of staff with regard to health and safety generally, and to emergency situations. Those named must have adequate information and authority to perform their responsibilities.

4 It is important that any likely hazards and the extent of health and safety matters under the employer's control are identified. Hazards can be listed, together with the rules and precautions for avoiding them and arrangements for dealing with injury, fire and other emergencies should be made clear. The arrangements for providing instruction, training and supervision should also be identified.

5 The general policy should be monitored and kept under review and the statement amended where necessary. The original statement and any subsequent revision must be brought to the notice of all employees. Newly recruited employees should not be overlooked.

6   Each employer should write their policy statement according to his or her own needs. It must be emphasised that the written word does not prevent accidents and it is the thorough implementation and application of an effective policy that can play an important part in accident prevention.

7   The priced HSE booklet *Writing your health and safety policy statement*[20] gives guidance on the preparation of a statement, laying out the important points using page by page examples.

APPENDIX 4: FACTORS/QUESTIONS WHEN MAKING AN ASSESSMENT OF MANUAL HANDLING OPERATIONS

Schedule 1 Factors to which the employer must have regard and questions he must consider when making an assessment of manual handling operations

Regulation 4(1)(b)(i)

Column 1 Factors	Column 2 Questions
1 The tasks	Do they involve: - holding or manipulating loads at distance from trunk? - unsatisfactory bodily movements or posture, especially: - twisting the trunk? - stooping? - reaching upwards? - excessive movement of loads, especially: - excessive lifting or lowering distances? - excessive carrying distances? - excessive pushing or pulling of loads? - risk of sudden movement of loads? - frequent or prolonged physical effort? - insufficient rest or recovery periods? - a rate of work imposed by a process?

2 The loads

Are they:
- heavy?
- bulky or unwieldy?
- difficult to grasp?
- unstable, or with contents likely to shift?
- sharp, hot or otherwise potentially damaging?

3 The working environment

Are there:
- space constraints preventing good posture?
- uneven, slippery or unstable floors?
- variations in level of floors or work surfaces?
- extremes of temperature or humidity?
- conditions causing ventilation problems or gusts of wind?
- poor lighting conditions?

4 Individual capability

Does the job:
- require unusual strength, height, etc?
- create a hazard to those who might reasonably be considered to be pregnant or to have a health problem?
- require special information or training for its safe performance?

5 Other factors

Is movement or posture hindered by personal protective equipment or by clothing?

APPENDIX 5: EXAMPLE FORM F2508 FOR REPORTING INJURIES AND DANGEROUS OCCURRENCES

Health and Safety Executive
Health and Safety at Work etc Act 1974
Reporting of Injuries, Diseases and Dangerous Occurrences Regulations 1985

Spaces below are for office use only

Report of an injury or dangerous occurrence

- Full notes to help you complete this form are attached.
- This form is to be used to make a report to the enforcing authority under the requirements of Regulations 3 or 6.
- Completing and signing this form does not constitute an admission of liability of any kind, either by the person making the report or any other person.
- If more than one person was injured as a result of an accident, please complete a separate form for each person.

A Subject of report *(tick appropriate box or boxes) — see note 2*

Fatality	Specified major injury or condition	"Over three day" injury	Dangerous occurrence	Flammable gas incident (fatality or major injury or condition)	Dangerous gas fitting
1	2	3	4	5	6

B Person or organisation making report (ie person obliged to report under the Regulations) — *see note 3*

Name and address —

Post code —

Name and telephone no. of person to contact —

Nature of trade, business or undertaking —

If in construction industry, state the total number of your employees —

and indicate the role of your company on site *(tick box)* —

Main site contractor 7   Sub contractor 8   Other 9

If in farming, are you reporting an injury to a member of your family? *(tick box)* Yes No

C Date, time and place of accident, dangerous occurrence or flammable gas incident — *see note 4*

Date [ ] [19] (day month year)   Time —

Give the name and address if different from above —

Where on the premises or site — and
Normal activity carried on there

ENV

Complete the following sections D, E, F & H if you have ticked boxes, 1, 2, 3 or 5 in Section A. Otherwise go straight to Sections G and H.

D The injured person — *see note 5*

Full name and address —

Age [ ]   Sex [ ] (M or F)   Status *(tick box)* — Employee 10   Self employed 11   Trainee (YTS) 12   Trainee (other) 13   Any other person 14

Trade, occupation or job title —

Nature of injury or condition and the part of the body affected —

F2508 (rev 1/86)   *continued overleaf*

APPENDIX 6: EXAMPLE FORM F2508A FOR REPORTING CASES OF DISEASES

HSE Health & Safety Executive

Health and Safety at Work etc Act 1974
Reporting of Injuries Diseases and Dangerous Occurrences Regulations 1985

For HSE use

Report of a case of disease

- This form is to be used to make a report to the enforcing authority under the requirements of Regulation 5.
- Completing and signing this form does not constitute an admission of liability of any kind, either by the person making the report or any other person.

A Person or organisation making report
(ie person obliged to report under the Regulations)

Name and address

Post code

Name of person to contact for further inquiry

Tel. No.

Nature of trade, business or undertaking

B Details of the person affected

Surname   Forenames

Date of birth [day] [month] 1 9 [year]   Sex (M or F)

Occupation

Please indicate whether   Employee ☐
(tick box)
                          Other person ☐

If not an employee, what is the ill person's status?
(eg self-employed or trainee)

F2508A (1/86)   continued overleaf

APPENDIX 7: USEFUL ADDRESSES AND CONTACTS

The British Horse Society
British Equestrian Centre
Stoneleigh Park
Kenilworth
Warwickshire
CV8 2LR

Tel: 0203 696697
Fax: 0203 692351

The Association of British Riding Schools
Old Brewery Yard
Penzance
Cornwall
TR18 2SL

Tel: 0736 69440

The Joint National Horse Education and Training Council
Northern Racing School
The Stables
Rossington Hall
Great North Road
Doncaster
South Yorkshire
DN11 0HN

Tel: 0302 865462

Local Authority Enforcement Officers (addresses and telephone numbers will be in your local telephone directories)

REFERENCES AND FURTHER READING

References

1 *Management of health and safety at work* Management of Health and Safety at Work Regulations 1992. Approved Code of Practice HSE Books ISBN 0 11 886330 4

2 *Manual handling* Manual Handling Operations 1992. Guidance on regulations HSE Books ISBN 0 11 886335 5

3 *Guide to the Reporting of Injuries, Diseases and Dangerous Occurrences Regulations 1985* HS(R)23 1986 HSE Books ISBN 0 11 883858 X

4 *First aid at Work: Health and Safety (First Aid) Regulations 1981* Approved Code of Practice and Guidance COP 42 1990 HSE Books ISBN 0 11 885536 0

5 *COSHH A brief guide for employers. The requirements of the Control of Substances Hazardous to Health (Regulations) 1988* IND(G)136(L) 1993 HSE Free leaflet

6 *Control of Substances Hazardous to Health and Control of Carcinogenic Substances.* Control of Substances Hazardous to Health Regulations 1988. Approved Codes of Practice (4th ed) 1993 HSE Books ISBN 0 11 882085 0

7 *Respiratory sensitisers: a guide for employers* IND(G)95(L) 1990 HSE Free leaflet

8 *Veterinary Medicines: safe use by farmers and other animal handlers* HS(G)86 1992 HSE Books ISBN 0 11 886361 4

9 *Workplace health, safety and welfare*. Workplace (Health, Safety and Welfare) Regulations 1992. Approved Code of Practice 1992 HSE Books ISBN 0 11 886333 9

10 *Personal protective equipment at work* Personal Protective Equipment at Work Regulations 1992. Guidance on regulations HSE Books ISBN 0 11 886334 7

11 BS 6473: 1984 *Protective hats for horse and pony riders*

12 BS 4472: 1988 *Protective skull caps for jockeys*

13 BS 6863: 1989 *Specification for pedal cyclist helmets*

14 BS 7671: 1992 Institution of Engineering *Regulations for Electrical Installations* (16th ed) 1991 ISBN 0 852965 57 5

15 *Memorandum of guidance on the Electricity at Work Regulations 1989* HS(R)25 1989 HSE Books ISBN 0 11 883963 2

16 *Safe use of portable electrical apparatus (electrical safety)* PM 32(rev) 1990 HSE Books ISBN 0 11 885590 5

17 *Flexible leads, plugs, sockets etc* GS 37 1985 HSE Books ISBN 0 11 883519 X

18 *Maintenance of portable electrical equipment* SS 28 1993 HSE Free information sheet

19 *Electrical Hazards from steam/water pressure cleaners etc* PM 29 (rev) 1988 HSE Books ISBN 0 11 883538 6

20 *Writing your health and safety policy statement* ISBN 0 11 883882 2

British Standards are available from:
British Standards Institution
Linford Wood
Milton Keynes MK14 6LE
Tel: 0908 220022   Fax: 0908 320856

Further reading

A step by step guide to COSHH assessment HS(G)97 1993
HSE Books ISBN 0 11 886379 7

Do you use a steam/water pressure cleaner? IND(G)68(L) 1989 HSE Free leaflet

Essentials of health and safety at work (rev) 1990
HSE Books ISBN 0 11 885445 3

Farmer's lung AS (5)(rev) 1988 HSE Free leaflet

Getting to grips with manual handling IND(G)143(L)   HSE Free leaflet

Guide to the Health and Safety at Work etc Act 1974 L1 (rev) 1990 HSE Books ISBN 0 11 885555 7

Handling and stacking bales in agriculture IND(G)125(L) 1992 HSE Free leaflet

Health and Safety at Work etc Act: advice to employees HSC5 1991 HSE Free leaflet

Health and Safety at Work etc Act: advice to employers HSC3 1990 HSE Free leaflet

It's your job to manage safety IND(G)103(L) 1991 HSE Free leaflet

Lighten the load: guidance for employees on musculoskeletal disorders IND(G)110(L) 1991 HSE Free leaflet

Lighten the load: guidance for employers on musculoskeletal disorders IND(G)109(L) 1991 HSE Free leaflet

New health and safety at work regulations IND(G)124(L) 1992 HSE Free leaflet

Pesticides: Code of Practice for the safe use of pesticides on farms and holdings HSE Books ISBN 0 11 242892 4

Power take-off and power take-off shafts AS 24 1984 HSE Free leaflet

Preventing accidents to children in agriculture: approved code of practice and guidance notes COP 24 1988 HSE Books ISBN 0 11 883997 7

Prevention of tractors overturning AS 22(rev) 1988 HSE Free leaflet

Reporting under RIDDOR HSE 24 1992 HSE Free leaflet

Respiratory protective equipment: a practical guide for users HS(G)53 1990 HSE Books ISBN 0 11 885522 0

Respiratory Protective Equipment: Legislative requirements and lists of HSE approved standards and type approved equipment (3rd ed) 1992 HSE Books ISBN 0 11 886382 7

Safety Threshold picture guide series no 14 1989 Kenilworth Press Ltd ISBN 0 901366 89 7

Safety Representatives and Safety Committees (as amended by the Management of Health and Safety at Work Regulations 1992) COP 1 HSE Books ISBN 0 11 883959 4

The stable yard. Manual of stable management 1989 British Horse Society Kenilworth Press Ltd ISBN 1 872082 28 9

Storage of approved pesticides: guidance for farmers and other professional users CS19 1988 HSE Books ISBN 0 11 885406 2

Successful health and safety management HS(G)65 1991 HSE Books ISBN 0 11 885988 9

Tractor-trailer safety brakes AS 16(rev) 1988 HSE Free leaflet

Watch your step: prevention of slipping, tripping and falling accidents at work 1985 HSE Books ISBN 0 11 883782 6

Writing a policy statement: advice to employers HSC6 (rev) 1987 HSE Free leaflet

Writing your health and safety policy statement: guide to preparing a safety policy statement for a small business (rev) 1989 HSE Books ISBN 0 11 885510 7